Presented To

_____

From

_____

Date

_____

Published in association with Eames Literary Services, Nashville, Tennessee.

NAVPRESS, BRINGING TRUTH TO LIFE, and the NAVPRESS logo are
registered trademarks of NavPress. Absence of ® in connection with marks of
NavPress or other parties does not indicate an absence of registration of those marks.

ISBN 1-57683-644-4

Cover and interior design by DeAnna Pierce, Russ McIntosh, Bill Chiaravalle
Brand Navigation, LLC — www.brandnavigation.com
Creative Team: Arvid Wallen, Rachelle Gardner, Darla Hightower

Printed in China
1 2 3 4 5 6 7 8 9 10 / 08 07 06 05 04

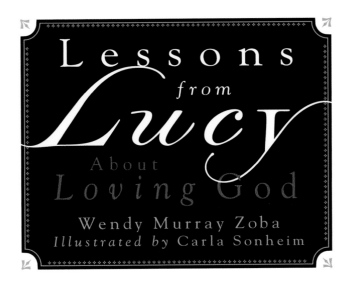

Lessons
from
Lucy
About
Loving God

Wendy Murray Zoba
Illustrated by Carla Sonheim

NAVPRESS ®

BRINGING TRUTH TO LIFE

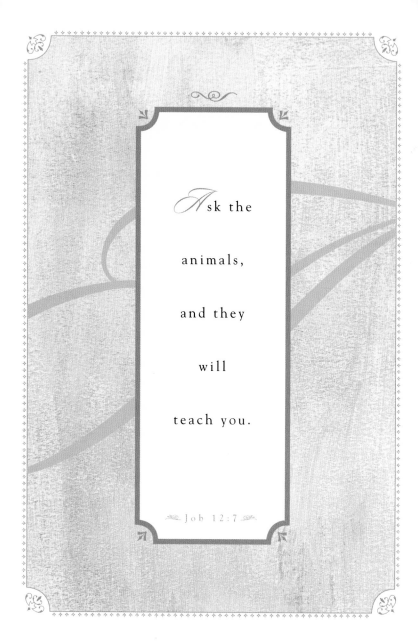

Ask the

animals,

and they

will

teach you.

Job 12:7

*H*ow do you ask for prayer for a dog? I almost did it one time during the summer of 1998. I was working full-time, and during staff devotions on a Monday morning, prayer requests were taken and I almost said, "I'd like prayer for my dog. His name is Bilbo. He's dying." The words were in my throat. But I left them there in deference to more rational requests relating to upcoming surgeries, travel mercies, and the like. Indeed our dog died that summer, our beloved Bilbo, a black Labrador retriever, after only eight years. A degenerative arthritic condition had made him too weak to lift his hundred-pound frame from the floor where he slept. I was shocked at how grief-stricken I was to lose him. We had almost lost him two times before, when we were living in Honduras. The first time, as a four-month-old puppy, he had escaped out the front gate, left open by our Honduran gardener. He was missing for three days. The second time, I was standing on the sidewalk chatting with a friend when Bilbo bolted out that same gate straight into an oncoming car. He survived both harrowing experiences and lived to sire two litters with his beloved "wife," Bonnie, a Honduran black Lab to whom Bilbo remained monogamous, despite others' attempts to benefit from his AKC pure bloodline.

I still miss him. As dogs do, he gave our family the constancy of his presence, his undemanding demeanor, and his desire only to please. I am crushed when I think of how many times I'd walk into the house to see him wagging his tail, hoping to be petted and spoken to, and I'd walk past him consumed by other distractions. Even so, he'd wait and receive me enthusiastically when I would remember to stop the next time. If ever a living creature exhibited aspects of a soul, that dog did in his devotion, his forbearance, his desire to impart pleasure, and in his joy in being with us.

Since then, I've met Lucy, a Lab with a touch of Boykin Spaniel that curls the fur on the edges of her ears. Lucy and I share a deep and mysterious bond.

When it comes to our ability to understand one another, I'm tempted to wonder if Lucy isn't one of God's surprise extraordinary, mystical reinforcements. She seems a ministering spirit to me. Once during a hard time, I ended up alone in my room in a heap of tears. Lucy, unbidden, came to me and licked them away. At other points during that dark time, she'd come by and sit near enough to rub up against me and warm my feet.

There is power in that kind of presence. I believe many dogs are ministering spirits. I believe they have lessons to share, if we allow ourselves eyes to see them and a mind to perceive the hidden possibilities behind commonplace moments. They see things. They feel the breath of God in their faces. Lucy shows me that God is here and that I can love him as Lucy loves me, if I give her a chance to show me the way.

He knows

his horses and dogs

as we cannot know them.

George MacDonald

L ucy taught me how to face a new day. She stepped out of her bed, nudging her head toward me (noting my presence), then chose her spot and sat. She turned her head, alerting me to her readiness. She waited for me to kneel next to her and place my fingers at the nape of her neck to begin the vigorous finger movements up and down her back. Once we'd done that, she turned again to lick my face, thanking me, then rose and started to sniff. She pressed her nose to the door, turned, and cocked her head. She paced the floor and sniffed a second time at the door. She was ready to meet the day. She was inviting me to meet it with her.

Seeing her undertake the same ritual with ease and satisfaction morning after morning, I realized my days didn't begin quite like that. In fact, there have been days when issues of heart and mind had left me unsure of which way to turn in the morning when the moment had come to arise.

Paul says our lives are "earthly tents" and that sometimes we groan and moan. Yet Paul prods us to press on, despite the groaning, under the hope that we have a promise heavenward. The Spirit will get us there, he says, directing those groans and moans in an upward ascent. Sometimes the "earthly tent" feels like covers and sheets on a day I'd rather go back to sleep. But Lucy nudges her nose toward me, and it has a way of pulling me from my bed. Those times when the groans and moans might otherwise win the day, I think about those nudges of her nose, and I think again about the Holy Spirit's nudging me as if to say, "Remember my presence."

Lucy's little nudges, of course, lead to her back rub. She turns her head to signal she's ready, sits and waits, and will not move until my fingers have worked their magic over her back. Seeing this, I think, perhaps if I lifted my face and turned toward God and waited, he'd incline himself to me. Perhaps, I think, when God comes near, even as I kneel next to Lucy to rub her back, his nearness will move me in a magical kind of way, just as my finger movements settle and satisfy Lucy.

So I arise with a nose toward God. I pick my spot and wait for him to meet me, and I will not retreat until I have felt his vigorous action work over me. Sometimes I feel it in the singing of a psalm. Sometimes I feel it when I pray from a prayer book. Sometimes I feel it when I speak the Lord's Prayer aloud. Sometimes I think he is saying to me, "Don't be afraid. Your pastures are green," and so I am satisfied.

Lucy starts sniffing. She's ready to go get the day. She moves toward the door. She paces the floor. She turns to me as if to say, "Well?" and I say, "Well, what?" It's as if she's saying to me, "Why are you standing there? Put on your walking shoes. There's a brand-new day out there. Let's go get it."

Lucy rises from her bed and

arches her back to stretch her haunches.

She turns her head to me.

She is waiting for a back rub.

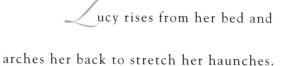

Each morning

I bring my requests
to you and wait
expectantly.

Psalm 5:3

$\mathcal{I}$ stroke her velvet ears,
and she lifts her nose to
lick my chin. She is saying,
"Thank you."

*T*ell God

what you

need, and

thank him

for all he

has done.

Philippians 4:6

*A*nimals, too, praise you.

For our souls lean for support

upon the things which you

have created, so that we

may be lifted up to you

from our weakness.

St. Augustine

*L*ucy and I took a walk on a mountain trail called "Craggy." It is full of odd twists, jagged rocks, and steep, jutting ledges. It's not as scary as it sounds. It's an easy walk to the top, but once you get there, you can find some hidden challenges.

We made it to the summit where on a clear day you can see the beautiful Smoky Mountains all the way into Tennessee. We were tired and hungry when we landed there. We found benches placed to welcome weary hikers. But Lucy wasn't inclined to sit by a bench. She sniffed and explored rocky ledges.

We stepped over the man-made stone wall barrier that enclosed the bench-sitters and found a comfortable nook on rocks overlooking the valley. We sat in the sun and ate our lunches. She drank water from a bottle poured into her lapping jowls. Then the adventure began.

I had the advantage of height, weight, and center of gravity. I could see how deep the canyon was and the distance to the lower ledge. I had the benefit of limbs with digits that could clutch rocks and roots in case of a slip. From the ledge where I stood, I could see that it was safe to explore the lower face. I climbed over and called Lucy. She hesitated. Her field of vision was only a few feet. She couldn't see what I knew to be the safe landing spot to which I summoned her.

"There is no bottom to that precipice," she seemed to be saying in halting sniffs and padding of front paws. "Come on, girl," I said. She fussed. She wanted to come and she moved a paw this way, and that. But she felt afraid. "Come on, Lu. You can do it." She retreated a half step, reoriented her footing, and finally came forth, albeit by a slightly different route than a direct leap. Her feet landed squarely and we went on our way.

I find astounding a simple passage from Mark's gospel: "One day Jesus came forth from Nazareth in Galilee and was baptized by John in the Jordan River" (1:9). That tells me that there was a day on the calendar when God stepped into the human arena. It involved mud. And water. And a riverbank. And hometown friends.

Jesus got wet. He put his feet in the mud. He led the way for the rest of us to get wet and put our feet in the mud. When he began his work and summoned his friends to come along, he went to where they were: to a shoreline, or a tax office. Pebbles crunched underfoot when he called the fishermen. They lifted their heads. They reoriented their footing. They followed.

Maybe they couldn't see where he was taking them. Maybe the precipice they neared seemed, to them, to have no bottom. They understood that was beside the point. They would be walking on the heels of the one they knew would not lead them off a cliff.

When we're on mountain trails where Lucy can see the path ahead, she likes to trot in front. Where ledges are steep and she can't see the next step, that slows her down and she waits for me. I pass her and turn to call. She follows. Not because she sees the way, but because she knows me. She knows I'll show her the next step.

She sniffs her leash,

ready for adventure.

She is willing to be led.

Then I heard

the Lord asking,

"Whom should I send as a

messenger to my people?

Who will go for us?"

And I said, "Lord,

I'll go! Send me."

Isaiah 6:8

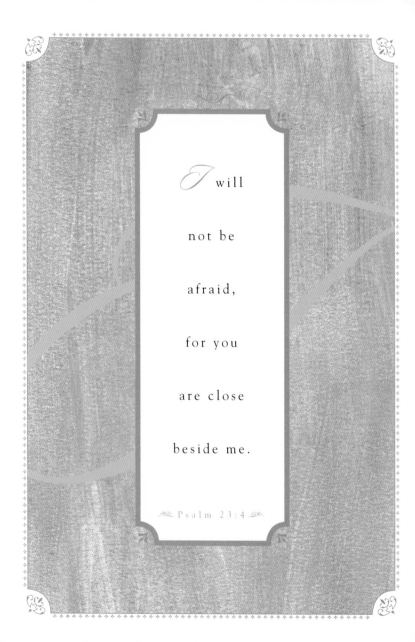

I will

not be

afraid,

for you

are close

beside me.

Psalm 23:4

Sometimes she's tentative and won't

walk through an open door.

Then she'll go forward with a little prodding

or a touch to the back of her neck.

Sometimes she's "Rodeo Dog"— spinning and spinning, 'round and 'round in circles, for the sheer joy of being ALIVE.

*Y*ou will
show me the
way of life,
granting me
the joy of
your presence
and the
pleasures of
living with
you forever.

$\mathscr{B}$rother Wolf, come here.
You wound God's creatures
without his permission, and not
only animals, but men made
in God's image. Everyone cries
out and murmurs against you.
But I wish to make peace
between you and the people.

St. Francis of Assisi

Sometimes Lucy looks foolish. Often before dinner, when my nephew James would play the harmonica, Lucy will sit at his feet, lift her chin, and begin to howl. Howling involves the kind of vocal-chord gymnastics that can be annoying. She hurls her voice to its outermost reaches, oblivious to any who might cringe at the dissonance.

When we visit the lake, she likes to play a game of retrieving a wet, spongy ball. It's a boring game. It involves picking up the ball and throwing it into the water. Lucy jumps into the water, paddles out to seize the ball in her mouth, then brings it back, dropping it at our feet, shaking off her own wetness, only to do it again. I'll throw it again and she'll jump again and swim again and retrieve it again and drop it at my feet again and shake again and look at us as if to say, "Again. And again. And again. And one more time, please."

I'll say, "Lucy! No more throwing balls! How can you find thrills time and time again over the same silly game? Stop this foolishness and find something else to do!"

Then she looks at me. It seems like she's saying, "But I like jumping into the lake. I like the wetness of water. I like to bring you the ball. Don't you like having the ball brought to you?"

St. Francis of Assisi used to talk to animals and never felt the fool. More to the point, they listened. He loved animals because to him they were God's special messengers, bearers of his secrets. In a small medieval town called Alviano, near Assisi, St. Francis had gone to the main plaza to preach. Rather than being surrounded by people, he was overtaken by swallows who made such a chatter about his being there, he could not speak. He said, "My sister swallows, it seems to me now that the time has come when I should have a chance to speak; now you have said enough. Hear therefore God's word and keep still and quiet while I preach." They ceased their chatter and obeyed. The foolishness of Francis' preaching to the birds, and their readiness to listen, ended up converting the people who'd gathered.

St. Francis looked foolish. But he carried God's humility in his heart and was willing to risk being the fool. He hurled his voice, even if only to fall upon the ears of swallows and larks and wolves. The animals loved him. The people finally did too. It reminds me of the apostle Paul, when he said God chooses the foolish things of this world to confound the wise. "God chose things despised by the world, things counted as nothing at all, and used them to bring to nothing what the world considers important" (1 Corinthians 1:28). Fools are his flag-bearers! They are his beginning point. They stand at the center of his holy purpose.

Next time James plays his harmonica, I am ready to join Lucy in her singing. I am ready to howl.

She howls at

the sounds of a harmonica playing.

(She is merciless.)

She is singing with angels.

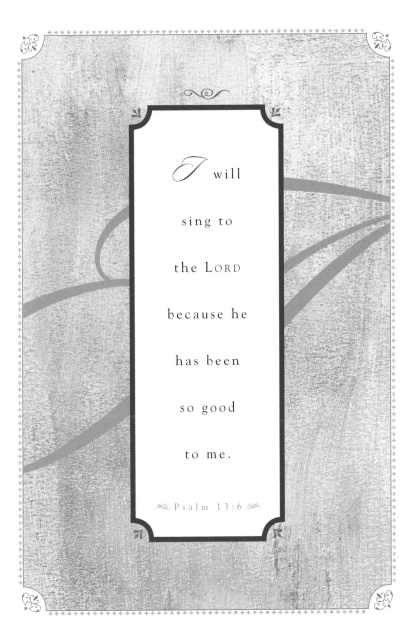

I will

sing to

the LORD

because he

has been

so good

to me.

Psalm 13:6

Be dressed for service
and well prepared,

as though you were

waiting for your master

to return . . .

Then you will be

ready to open the door

and let him in

the moment he arrives

and knocks.

Luke 12:35-36

She doesn't understand when you say,

"I'll play ball with you tomorrow."

There is only today.

Are you going to play ball?

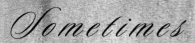

Sometimes

on walks

she'll bolt ahead.

Then she'll turn

to make sure

I'm there.

She follows

in front.

*R*un in such

a way that you

will win . . .

Run straight

to the goal

with purpose

in every step.

1 Corinthians
9:24,26

What I saw in his eyes was as
gracious a prayer as any I have
set down at the feet of Glory.
He asked nothing for himself or
for any of his four-footed kind,
but only that all should be
well with his master.

Frederick Buechner

Night

Late at night when I am already warm and reposed in my bed with a good book, sometimes Lucy will come and curl next to me. She'll jump on the bed, pad around with her feet, turn, then drop comfortably near my legs as I read, her head on my lap.

She sleeps placidly there and sighs now and then. When she does that, I think, *That's just how I feel — like it's been a long day and this bed feels good.*

Her warmth reaches me. She is at peace. She is not thinking about who will feed her tomorrow, or even if there will be food.

"He is the source of every mercy," Paul wrote, "and the God who comforts us" (2 Corinthians 1:3). "Every mercy" suggests there are more than one, that there are repeated mercies, and that through them God comforts us. He knows we need food and asks us not to worry about that. He wants us to curl up near and rest our heads and not fret about who will feed us tomorrow or if there will be food. He wants us to sigh and settle our tired hearts and receive the warmth of his presence, to nourish from the sweet wellspring of trust.

When it is time to turn out the light and Lucy must return to her own bed, she'll look at me and tilt her head and cock her ears. She doesn't understand why she can't sleep in the warmth of my bed. "We're such friends," she seems to say. "Why don't you want me leaning next to you all night?"

After the attacking Babylonians sacked and razed Jerusalem, sitting in its ruins Jeremiah said, "I am one who has seen the afflictions . . . He has brought me deep into darkness, shutting out all light" (Lamentations 3:1-2). He might as well have said, "God has left me for dead."

Jeremiah continues: "Yet I still dare to hope when I remember this: The unfailing love of the LORD never ends! . . . His mercies begin afresh each day" (Lamentations 3:21-23).

Three letters kept Jeremiah clinging to hope: Y- E -T. "Yet" is the look on Lucy's face when she tilts her head and cocks her ears and looks at me curiously as if she didn't understand.

It is the "yet" of Jeremiah's lament and of my heart's cry and of Lucy's deep sighing that gives rest without thoughts of the needs of another day, and we rise and go where we may not want to go, knowing that promises await us there.

"Praise the LORD, I tell myself," David says in a psalm (103). Sometimes we need reminding not only to praise, but to see God's gifts to us and to thank him. In that psalm David tells "armies of angels": "Praise the Lord for everything he has created everywhere in his kingdom." His gifts are everywhere.

Lucy, a gray-snouted, drooling, sometimes howling, sniffing, loping 60-pound chocolate Lab-Boykin mix is a gift. Sometimes I pass through the door where she greets me, tail sweeping, and I walk by. When I think of it, I'd be crushed except for this one thing: On the days I remember to stop and sit with her and rub her ears while she licks my face, it is as if the ignoring times had never happened. My being crushed would itself crush that dog. She's ready when the ear rubs finally come.

She rests with me,

her head on my lap.

She sighs in her sleep. Her soul is at rest.

She has nothing to bring but the

solace of her presence.

$\mathcal{I}$ will lie

down in peace

and sleep,

for you alone,

O LORD, will

keep me safe.

Psalm 4:8

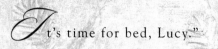

"It's time for bed, Lucy."

She tilts her head and perks her ears:

"Am I hearing you correctly?"

She walks to her bed and turns with pleading eyes:

"Do I have to?"

She turns again and

goes on anyway.

My heart has heard

you say, "Come and talk with me."

And my heart responds,

"LORD, I am coming."

Psalm 27:8

*F*rederick Buechner says a saint is "a life-giver." He says, "If a saint touches your life, you become alive in a new way." Does that make Lucy a saint? I can't say. I know only that every place she walks with me is her favorite place to be — and every ball she fetches, and every cliff she descends. She has a lot of favorite places: mountain trails and the dock at the lake; the wetness of water; the spot on the bed where she rests her head on my lap. She follows me, even when she'd rather not. She knows I'm there to bring the ball back to, and when she's afraid of the step, my voice is enough to rally courage. Her pleasure is her devotion. Her devotion is her praise. That is her gift to me.

In Memoriam,

for Bilbo (Wendy)

&

for Roxy (Carla)